A NEW SONG

Gary Wilson

CONTENTS

DEDICATION

This book is dedicated to my wife Helen, my three children: Andrew, Sarah, and Rachel. I thank the Lord for His grace and kindness by blessing me with your love and life. You are all a great joy to me and it is a privilege to be part of your lives. Love you all.

FOREWORD

I love this book. It's readable, engaging and really edifying. *A New Song* wasn't written by a book-worm for bookie people. It's a life's compendium of rich gleanings from a follower of Jesus with a keen ear for God's voice amid a thousand others, compiled through highs and lows common to many.

Gary's Bible is no academic treadmill. It's a jour-neyman's roadmap, rucksack and First Aid kit, rolled into one. Like the pastor-evangelist he is, Gary gathers 3,000-year old treasures from the Book of Psalms, observes them played out in human history, brings them to life through per-sonal anecdote, and offers them to you and me as from the Author Himself.

A New Song is the work of a winner of souls. Just like Gary does at weddings and funerals, on the football park or on community radio, this anthology takes Jesus into the 99% of your life that doesn't exist in a church building on Sunday mornings, and gives much greater sense of the 1% that does.

I've had the joy of partnering Gary in the Gospel for many years and, like others, I can easily recall moments when he blessed me. As I sit on this Glasgow-Euston train right now, I reflect on June 22nd, 2007, as I rushed home on the Euro Shuttle from Belgium, anxious to be at my late father's bedside before his passing. My phone rang late in the night. It was Gary, at Dad's bedside, exchanging messages of comfort between us both. You cannot put into words what these things mean.

The highest possible accolade I can give Gary is that my dad, Captain Matheson, a wise man of few words, spoke well of him. Only someone who truly understands the aversion of a Hebridean Gael to hyperbole and flattering speech, could possibly appreciate the weightiness my father's words when he took it upon himself one day, unprompted, to advise me: *"Gary is a good man."*

High praises indeed!

Gary is a good man. And this is a good book.

Alistair Matheson

Pastor, Glasgow City Church

September 2021

INTRODUCTION

I waited patiently for the Lord. He turned to me and heard my cry. He lifted me out of the slimy pit, out of the mud and mire; He set my feet on a rock and gave me a firm place to stand. He put a new song in my mouth, a hymn of praise to our God.

(Psalm 40:1-3)

The rock band U2 wrote a song called 40 which was based on Psalm 40 in the Bible. In fact, the lyrics are all taken from the Bible apart from the chorus which is a continual cry of, 'how long to sing this song.' In other words, how long must we wait, Lord? In this pit, in the mud and mire of sin. How long? This is a heart- felt cry as Northern Ireland at the time were going through troubles. This song made quite an impact on my life and later on in my journey, God would remind me of the words that ultimately brought me back to a relationship with Him.

My life started out in Possilpark in the north side of Glasgow. We lived in the tenements at Killearn Street in a one-bedroom flat. I was brought up in a close community living in the tenements, you went in and out of each other's flats. The doors were always open. However, things started to change with my friends, when we started school. On my first day at Saracen Primary, I was shocked to find that some of my friends were not there. At playtime I looked across at this big wire mesh fence and saw my friends.

They went to St Cuthbert's school and this massive fence divided us. We could talk through the fence to each other but could not play or learn together. I could not understand this and later that day some of the older boys would throw stones over the fence and call each other names. What a start to school.

About a week later as I was leaving school, I was grabbed by two big lads and they asked me: 'What are you?' I thought I was a boy! The questions kept coming: 'Are you a Cathy or a Proddy? Green or blue? Do you sing the sash or rebel song?'

I had no idea what they were talking about but I knew if I did not answer it to their liking I would be in for a kicking.

I said, 'I don't know! But I think I might be German!'

They looked at me in astonishment and to my relief they let me go!

I later found out from my parents that I was a Proddy and would be a blue and sing the sash! Which still meant nothing to me. What I did see at a young age is we lived in a divided city.

I thank God that when I cried out to Him for mercy, He placed my life on a solid foundation in Jesus and put a new song in my mouth, not the sash but a song of salvation. This new song took a while to develop in me and I am still a work in progress.

We left Possilpark in 1969 and moved to new high-rise flats in Milton and I attended a new school called Miltonbank Primary. One day before setting off for school, I had been warned by my mum not to go to the canal bank after school as it was dangerous. I assured her I would not go.

However, after school all my friends were heading for the canal as they were going to practice their running and jumping skills for the Olympic Games that we hoped to enter in the years to come. I thought, I cannot miss an opportunity such as this so I went to the forbidden place with my future Olympians.

When we arrived, the first event was to be the long jump, the challenge was to jump from one side of the canal bank over the water to the other side. One by one my friends attempted it and all managed the challenge, the last to go was me and I did not think that I was going to make it to the other side. However, there was no going back, I had to attempt it, I ran with all of my strength and jumped with all my might and almost got to the other side, but landed in the side of the bank which was like quicksand. I started to sink into this mud, my friends thought this was hilarious, but I was in trouble, I was going down.

I called out for them to help me, and eventually they grabbed a hold of me and pulled me out. I was relieved, but my legs and trousers were covered in mud up to above my knees and one of my shoes was missing! We tried to get the shoe back, but the mud closed in and we could not retrieve the shoe.

I had to walk home, which was about a mile away, with only one shoe on and covered in mud. Arriving at my home, mum came out and said, 'I know where you have been today; you have been to the canal, haven't you?' I answered, 'How do you know?' It was pretty obvious as I was covered in mud with only one shoe on!

As I reflect on that story and the words of Psalm 40, it encourages me that even in the most difficult and challenging times there is hope. The songwriter cried out to God for help in the pit and the mud and mire of life. He was going down and under, God heard his cry and lifted him out of the slime that was taking him down.

That day at the canal bank reminded me I was in trouble and I was going down, if I had not cried out for help, I could have gone under. I lost a shoe, and sometimes you have to leave things behind, or they will take you under, perhaps old bitter thoughts, negative attitudes, unhealthy lifestyle, wrong relationships or an unforgiving spirit.

Maybe you have no hope and are on a downward spiral, can I encourage you to cry out to God, the Maker of heaven and earth, the One who formed you, made you and loves you.

The songwriter, David, was going through a real difficult and trying time, even though he was a believer and a man after God's own heart, he still faced dark times, oppressive times and opposition from enemies within his camp and outwith his camp. In his distress he patiently waited upon the Lord, he did not run about trying to solve things, he did not struggle or thrash about for he was in a slimy pit, mud heap and if you thrash around in a mud heap you will go under. No! In the slimy pit of life's troubles he waited patiently upon the Lord and the Lord heard his cry.

"He lifted me from the slimy pit, out of the mud and mire; he set my feet upon a rock and gave me a firm place to stand. He put a new song in my mouth, a hymn of praise to our God. Many will see and fear and put their trust in the Lord." (Psalm 40:2-3)

It is this 'new song' that I would like to look at in this book, focusing on a wealth of songs written in the Bible which are words sung, by many, who found themselves in challenging times on their life journey but were given a 'new song' in all of their different life experiences and seasons.

I hope you will know the blessing of the Lord, as you read about some of these songs and that they may be a catalyst to bring about a 'new song' in your mouth in the days ahead.

As Bono of U2, sang, on numerous occasions: 'I will sing, sing a new song.' It is a new song that gives us hope. A new song is like an anthem to our soul. A new song is for all occasions and times in life and I hope you join in with me by belting it out. For how long? I believe for as long as we live and until we are in glory, joining in with the heavenly choir. Revelation 5:9 *'And they sang a new song!'*

CHAPTER 1. A LOVE SONG. PSALM 51

Part of my upbringing included Friday night parties, where my dad's side of the family would visit us for a drinking and singing session some Fridays. These started out being good fun and lots of laughs as each of us in turn began singing; anything from Johnny Cash to Frank Sinatra. This continued into my teenage years when I would get together with my friends for Friday night sessions, inevitably we ended up drinking too much and singing too loud.

The Proddy boys would sing the sash and the Cathy boys the rebel song and then our final rendition together would be: 'I belong to Glasgow, dear old Glasgow toon.' Even in our differences we seemed to get together again. Yet for many there was not too much love shown or even sung about unless it was a Beatles song or Jennifer Rush.

Some songs can have a divisive effect on communities and others a unifying anthem bringing people together.

This 'new song' that a believer in Jesus sings is an anthem of love. It brings people, communities and nations together. It is what we all crave as human beings is to be loved and to love someone. Many new songs that have been written and are in the process of being composed are about love. And why not? Someone said, 'That love is the greatest thing.'

The Beatles wrote; 'All you need is love. Love is all you need!' I don't think too many people would argue with that.

What is love?

We only have one English word for love. We may love a new pair of shoes. We may love fish and chips. We may fall in love. We may love a movie, song or band. For some, love means soppy sentimental warm feelings for another. But is that love?

The Greek language has four different words and meanings for love. Philia – friendship bond. Eros – romantic love. Storge – empathy bond. Agape – unconditional "God" love.

God's word has all these meanings of love woven through its pages. There are many love songs in the Psalms. Before we look at one, I want to take you to a love poem which the Apostle Paul wrote to the church at Corinth.

Love is patient, love is kind.

It does not envy, it does not boast, it is not proud.

It is not rude, it is not self-seeking, it is not easily angered, it keeps no record of wrongs.

Love does not delight in evil but rejoices with the truth.

It always protects, always trusts, always hopes, always perseveres.

Love never fails...

And now these three remain: faith, hope and love.

But the greatest of these is love.

(1 Corinthians 13)

At the heart of the songs of the Bible is the heart of love from the great inspirational composer the Holy Spirit, who comes alongside and within the mind and heart of King David who was the writer and singer of many of these songs.

David was aware of God's great love for him, as he struggled with his sin and shortcomings. In one account he had committed adultery with Bathsheba and sent her husband Uriah to the front line where the fighting was at its fiercest, and he was killed.

Through the revelation of the prophetic word to him, he realized that he had done wrong and he was full of guilt and remorse. It is in that state he sings out, cries out to God, for mercy.

"Have mercy on me, O God, according to your unfailing love; according to your great compassion blot out my transgressions. Wash away all my iniquity and cleanse me from my sin... Create in me a pure heart, O God and renew a steadfast spirit within me. Do not cast me from your presence or take your Holy Spirit from me." (Psalm 51:1-2, 10-11)

The Hebrew word for love is 'Ahavah' and it has a few meanings. Ahavah is care that one person shows to another, it can be parental love, brotherly love, friendship. God's Ahavah for His people is akin to that of a husband and wife, or a parent and child. He loves because He loves! It is his character to love. His Ahavah love is shown not just in His affection and feelings for His people but also as an action, an outworking of His love.

"The Lord did not set His affection on you and choose you because you were more numerous than other peoples, for you were fewest of all peoples. But it was because the Lord loved you and kept the oath, he swore to your forefathers that he brought you out with a mighty hand and redeemed you from the land of slavery." (Deuteronomy 7:7-8)

It is in God's nature to love. God is love. We love because He first loved us. His love is unconditional; it knows no bounds. *"God demonstrates his own love for us in this: While we were still sinners, Christ died for us."* (Romans 5:8)

All through history God has demonstrated His love through creation, through covenant promises to Noah, Abraham, Isaac and Jacob. He has been slow to anger and full of compassion. David penned a song to Almighty God for His great love towards him and all people with these powerful verses taken from Psalm 145: 8-9, 13, 17-18.

"The Lord is gracious and compassionate, slow to anger and rich in love. The Lord is good to all; he has compassion on all he has made... The Lord is faithful to all his promises and loving towards all he has made... The Lord is righteous in all his ways and loving towards all he has made. The

Lord is near to all who call on him, to all who call on him in truth."

The greatest love song ever written was a song that comes from the very heart and being of God for His people: *"For God so loved the world, that he gave his only begotten son, that whosoever believes in him should not perish but have eternal life."* (John 3:16). What a love song! An anthem of love down through the ages culminating in the saving work of Jesus.

'I stand amazed in the presence of Jesus the Nazarene and wonder how he could love me, a sinner, condemned unclean? How marvelous! How wonderful! And my song shall ever be. How marvelous and how wonderful is my Saviour's love for me!' (Charles Hutchinson Gabriel 1856-1932).

CHAPTER 2. BLUES SONG. PSALM 137

"By the rivers of Babylon, we sat and wept when we remembered Zion." (Psalm 137:1)

The birth of the blues song and music took place in the Southern States of the USA from the late 19th century, its musical influence is taken from Africa. African enslaved people brought their musical traditions with them when they were transported to work in the North American colonies. Early types of African American music included spirituals (religious songs using vocal harmony) and work songs. Enslaved people would sing work songs while working the plantations and religious spirituals in church. Combined with African rhythms, these musical styles were the foundation of the blues. Much of these early spiritual songs were based on the Psalms of lament, and those African believers who were enslaved could relate to the Bible and the stories of the enslaved Hebrew people of the Old Testament who lived under the brutal rule of the Pharaoh of Egypt. The Hebrews were also on many occasions exiled from their homeland and were refugees in other oppressive nations and rulers.

Songs, such as Psalm 137, were developed in a foreign land under slavery of a tyrannical king and his nation. These songs were original blues and were a longing and crying out to God for better times and time of deliverance! These songs are as appropriate today as they were hundreds and thousands of years ago. We all have our moments of 'blues' and it is amazing how a song from such a place in your life can give you hope and inner strength in a God who is with you in the hard and sad times, as well as the good and glad times.

As a minister of the gospel one of the saddest and hardest things I have to do are funeral services, some are sadder than others. I have been at funerals when there were only three people present, me and the two undertakers. I have buried a young girl, who had not lived long enough to attend primary school. A young man at the prime of his life playing football and dropping dead during a game, a young woman in a car accident where her car swerved off road and she died. Tragic, raw, tough, awful, numb, faith challenging, to name but a few emotions I was experiencing, but the overall emotion was sadness, almost uncontrollable grief. Life is tough, there are a lot of things we cannot explain and we cannot give any glib answers to, and we have to be honest with people that we don't always understand why these things happen, but we want you to know that we are there with you in this time of grief.

"Rejoice with those who rejoice; mourn with those who mourn." (Romans 12:15)

The Bible is full of broken people and stories of great distress and grief. There are cries from the heart of people who are mourning. There are many in distress at the fall of the nation and the spiritual backslide of people. There are times when the people of Israel were exiled from their homes and land and weeping and lamenting by the rivers of Babylon in a foreign land cut off from their homes. Jesus was overwhelmed with grief and deeply troubled almost to the point of death. He began to be deeply distressed and troubled. *"My soul is overwhelmed with sorrow to the point of death."* (Mark 14:34). Jesus cried out from the cross: *"My God, My God, why have you forsaken me?"* (Matthew 27:46)

There are many 'blues' songs in the Psalms, we may think that they are all negative and do not have much hope or encouragement to them. We could not be further from the truth, the fact is that these sad songs are real expressions of how someone is feeling, as you see, in times of great joy there are also times of great sorrow.

"Those who sow in tears will reap with songs of joy. He who goes out weeping, carrying seed to sow, will return with songs of joy, carrying sheaves with him." (Psalm 126:5-6). These songs give us hope because there are times when we feel lonely, isolated, broken, forgotten, and misunderstood! Times where we have lost a loved one, lost a relationship and have felt so down we want to give up.

"Why are you downcast O my soul, why so disturbed within? Put your hope in God for I will yet praise him my Saviour and my God." (Psalm 43:5)

Did you know that Jesus cried out words and songs of lament (blues)? His emotions were moved at the death of his friend Lazarus, it says in John 11:35 that 'Jesus wept.' At the Garden of Gethsemane before facing the cross; He began to be deeply distressed and troubled.

"My soul is overwhelmed with sorrow to the point of death."

From the very cross He sang a song of the blues: *"My God, my God why have you abandoned me? Why are you so far from saving me, so far from the words of my groaning? O my God, I cry out by day, but you do not answer, by night, and am not silent."* (Psalm 22:1-2)

Have you ever felt distressed and troubled? Have you felt alone and abandoned and in despair? At some point in our lives, we all experience the pain of sorrow, distress, trouble and abandonment and it sucks! Is there hope? Will we ever sing a new song?

It is alright to feel like this at times. It's alright to cry out to God. I remember when I was younger my parents would try to hide death from me. They felt that they were protecting me and when I first experienced the passing of my beloved grandmother, I did not know what to do.

I had many feelings of anger, distress, guilt, numbness and overwhelming grief. We never talked about it, bottled it up, kept the stiff upper lip. The writers of the Psalms do not bottle it up; they let it all out. How they feel, they shout, sing, cry, be still, and ask questions to God. Is that not a healthy way to lament? The psalmist reminds us, 'that weeping may endure for a night but joy comes in the morning.' In other words when you let go of all your emotions, let it all out, a time will come when you will know joy again but if you bottle everything up you may become depressed, bitter and angry which is not good for our wellbeing. There is a powerful

hymn written by Philip. P. Bliss, which is one of lament
and also of joy.

Man of sorrows what a name

For the Son of God who came

Ruined sinners to reclaim:

Hallelujah, what a Saviour!

Bearing shame and scoffing rude,

In my place condemned he stood,

Sealed my pardon with his blood:

Hallelujah, what a Saviour!

He was lifted up to die;

"It is finished" was his cry;

Now in heaven exalted high:

Hallelujah, what a Saviour!

Songs of sorrow (blues) allow us to express how we feel,
they allow us not to bottle things up but to let it out and,
in the time ahead they can help us in the grieving and

healing process.

CHAPTER 3. A SABBATH SONG. PSALM 92

The only song in the psalter which is called a song for the Sabbath day is Psalm 92 which opens with the words:

"It is good to praise the Lord and make music to your name, O Most High, to proclaim your love in the morning and your faithfulness at night, to the music of the ten-stringed lyre and the melody of the harp. For you make me glad by your deeds, O Lord; I sing for joy at the work of your hands."

Wow! For a Sabbath day song there is a great amount of rejoicing and the playing of the musical instruments on the Sabbath. It is joyous because the Sabbath day is meant to be one of rest and not enforced restrictions. Our focus is to be upon the one who is God the Creator whose works of creation over a period of six days ended with the seventh day being a day of rest. Oh how people need a day of rest, oh how society needs a day of rest.

I know like most people when I am about to have a day off, I am pretty happy and looking forward to it. That is why the psalmist begins the song with his focus on God and His goodness to us. He praises the Lord and makes music to the Lord. He is glad about the works of the Lord, looking at the Creator's creation, mountains, vegetation, animals, food, moon, sun, stars and humanity. He is in awe! and sings for joy at the work of the

Lord's hands.

The Sabbath day is meant to be a joyful day, a day to take time out, to be still and know that He is God. To spend time with family and friends and to worship the Lord for He is good and His love endures forever. Sabbath rest and Sabbath singing to the Lord are restorative and can give longevity.

Look at the climax of the song: *"The righteous will flourish like a palm tree, they will grow like a Cedar of Lebanon; planted in the house of the Lord, they will flourish in the courts of our God. They will still bear fruit in old age; they will stay fresh and green."*

Too many people in today's society are overworked, overstressed, and every minute of the day seems to be consumed with deadlines. Many suffer anxieties, stress-related illnesses, burn out, stomach ulcers and a list of many other ailments because they have not been able to take time out. Everyone needs a rest. It is built into our DNA and if we do not rest at least one day in seven we can shorten our life span. God is no killjoy He built into creation a day of rest; He wants it to be a delight to you; not religious or an imposition of rules and rituals but to be a refreshing, restorative and reviving day. Psalm 23: *"The Lord is my shepherd I shall not be in want. He makes me lie down in green pastures, he leads me beside still waters, he restores my soul."*

Leonardo da Vinci said a wise thing: 'Every now and then go away, have a little relaxation, for when you come back to your work your judgement will be surer, since to remain constantly at work will cause you to lose power of judgement... Go some distance away because then the work appears smaller, and more of it can be taken in at a glance, and lack of harmony or proportion is more readily seen.'

In 2005, National Geographic published the findings of scientists, who travelled around the globe to learn the secrets of longevity from populations that had high rates of centenarians, few deadly diseases, and more healthy years of life. Among them were people who kept the Sabbath day and scientists pointed to their practice of Sabbath as one of the reasons for their good health. These findings are surely in line with what the psalmist sung in this one and only Sabbath song in the psalter: *"They will still bear fruit in their old age, they will stay fresh and green, proclaiming, 'The Lord is upright; he is my Rock, and there is no wickedness in him.'"*

The Sabbath day observance has many benefits, our mental health and well-being, taking time from the hustle and bustle of life to be still. Whether you are a believer or not we are all created with a need to rest, one day in seven, if we don't, we get tired, irritable and in danger of burning out. The Sabbath is a gift from God to bless His people with rest and refreshment. If it was good enough for the Creator then it should be good enough for us. It has been noted throughout Jewish history that the Jewish people tried to keep the Sabbath in every place that they were dispersed to and in every ungodly circumstance that they found themselves in. Someone said, 'it was the Sabbath that kept the Jews!'

GARY WILSON

Jesus said, *"The Sabbath was made for man, not man for the Sabbath. So, the Son of man is Lord even of the Sabbath."* (Mark 2:27-28)

The Sabbath was intended to help people not burden them. For someone to forbid acts of mercy and goodness on God's day of rest is contrary to all that is right. It is the Sabbath that keeps us. For Jesus is Lord of the Sabbath and He wants the very best for your wellbeing. It is crucial that you build into your week a day of rest, for if you do not build into your week Sabbath rest times, you are in danger of cracking up and falling apart!

There is a hymn written by Horatius Bonar that draws us to find Sabbath rest in our relationship with Jesus.

I heard the voice of Jesus say,

'Come unto me and rest.

Lay down, O weary one,

Lay down your head upon my breast.'

I came to Jesus as I was,

So weary, worn, and sad.

I found in him a resting place,

And he has made me glad.

"If you call the Sabbath a delight and the Lord's holy day honourable, and if you honour it by not going your own way and not doing as you please or speaking idle words, then you will find joy in the Lord." (Isaiah 58:13-14)

The Sabbath is not to be legalistic and restrictive; it is to be liberating and restorative in us as individuals and among our families and communities in which we live.

CHAPTER 4. THE SHEPHERD'S SONG. PSALM 23

One of the most famous songs in the Bible is Psalm 23 which had become known in Scotland as the Scottish psalm although it was written by King David somewhere in the land of Israel. It is known as the Scottish psalm because it was a very popular song which was mostly sung at funeral services, worship services, and schools throughout the land in the days gone by. I can understand why it was sung at many funeral services as the words gave hope and assurance, but if we sing it only on this occasion then we miss out on the blessing of the Shepherd's song which can be sung on all occasions.

It is a very personal song between the shepherd and his God. David, the author, sings: 'The Lord is my shepherd.' That is personal. It is not an airy-fairy view of God as a being somewhere out in the heavens. This God is personal, so much so that David writes about the intimacy he has with his God. He has a wonderful personal relationship with him. This God wants a personal relationship with people. A real living relationship. Not just a religious belief, but a heart and mind moving relationship with his people.

Let us look at these first few verses 1 to 3. "*The Lord is my shepherd, I shall not be in want. He makes me lie down in green pastures, he leads me beside quiet waters, he restores my soul. He guides me in the paths of righteousness for his name's sake."*

This shepherd wants the very best for his flock. He provides for his people so that they will not be in need. (Look at the Lord's Prayer). Both physical and spiritual needs are provided for. He feeds the hungry and satisfies the thirsty. He gives rest and shalom to His people that they may be restored mentality, emotionally and spiritually. The shepherd takes care of his flock. Jesus said, *"I am the good shepherd; I know my sheep and my sheep know me – just as the Father knows me and I know the Father – and I lay down my life for the sheep."* (John 10:14)

I reflect back to an occasion when I was an assistant minister in Portree for 15 months. I had moved from the city of Edinburgh, and had been a city boy all of my life, now I was moving to the pretty remote and rural Island of Skye. My wife and I were living in a croft house with our new born baby son, Andrew. Not long into my ministry, Andy MacPherson, who owned our rented croft house, was also a crofter and shepherd and was an elder in our congregation, he invited me one day to come with him to find the 'lost sheep.' I thought he was having me on. We set out early in the morning to find this lost sheep and left the other sheep in the field. We were out for about two hours before we spotted this straggly, dirty sheep who had not been sheared for over a year. It was a stubborn old sheep and did not want to come back but the shepherd, Andy never gave up trying to rescue it. Eventually we got it to come back with some other sheep and we made it back to the flock. Andy was delighted, so happy that he found his lost sheep and managed to bring it back home. Then, Andy asked me to hold this sheep for him to shear it. I said that I had never held a sheep and was afraid that it might wriggle away from me and be lost forever. Thankfully I managed to hold on to it long enough for it to get a short back and sides! I was taught how much the shepherd loved his sheep, even the one.

On another occasion, I was out with Andy and he was checking his flock who were coming into the lambing season, he noticed that one was missing and we went looking for it and found it in a ditch very distressed and in labour, we managed to lift it out of the ditch, get it into the back of the van and it gave birth to a lamb. Andy showed me something about the nature of God. How the shepherd cares for his flock, even the lost ones, even the ones who fall into a pit, he never gives up on them. Just like Jesus the Good Shepherd who leaves the 99 behind, to find the one. Who cares for His flock, His rod and staff protect and guide them into the best places. The shepherd ultimately lays down his life for his flock.

This psalm of David, the Lord is my shepherd, reveals to us the heart of the Father. A heart of love, tender care, mercy and protection from the enemies. This song also reveals seven Hebrew names for God, which describe His character and His heart for his flock. One of the Hebrew words for God's name is Yahweh which means, 'My Lord.' Let us look at the seven phrases in the psalm that highlights His name.

1. 'I shall not want'- Yahweh Yireh, 'the Lord will provide.' (Genesis 22:14)

2. 'Still waters'- Yahweh Shalom, 'the Lord our peace.' (Judges 6:24)

3. 'Restores my soul' - Yahweh Rophe, 'the Lord who heals.'   (Exodus 15:26)

4. 'Paths of righteousness'-Yahweh Tsidkenu, 'the Lord our righteousness.' (Jeremiah 33:16)

5. 'You are with me'- Yahweh Shammah, 'the Lord is there.'   (Ezekiel 48:35)

6. 'Presence of my enemies'- Yahweh Nissi, 'the Lord is our banner.' (Exodus 15:15)

7. 'Anoint my head'- Yahweh M'Kaddesh, 'the Lord who sanctifies.' (Leviticus 20:8)

These are all attributes that our great shepherd king has! We can say like King David, 'The Lord is my shepherd, I have everything I need.' For He is MY Provider, My Peace, My Healer, My Righteousness, My Presence, My Banner, My Sanctifier, My all in all! Wow! There is a lot to know about our good shepherd. In fact, Jesus said of himself: *"I am the good shepherd; I know my sheep and my sheep know me... My sheep listen to my voice; I know them, and they follow me. I give them eternal life, and they shall never perish; no one can snatch them out of my hand."* (John 10:14, 27-28)

Henry Williams Baker (1868) wrote this powerful song based on Psalm 23.

The King of love my shepherd is, whose goodness faileth never,

I nothing lack if I am his, and he is mine forever.

Where streams of living water flow, my ransomed soul he leadeth,

And where the verdant pastures grow, with food celestial feedeth.

Perverse and foolish oft I strayed, but yet in love he sought me,

And on his shoulder gently laid, and home rejoicing, brought me.

And so, through all the length of days, thy goodness faileth never;

Good shepherd, may I sing thy praise, within thy house forever.

Psalm 23, the song of the shepherd is a prophetic psalm that spoke of the One who David had a relationship with, Yahweh, and that revelation would be shown to both Jew and Gentile in the years to come as Israel's Messiah and ours. Jesus, the good shepherd of His sheep who leads us into an everlasting kingdom, pictured as a house, *"In my Father's house are many rooms if it were not so I would have told and I go there to prepare a place for you that you may be where I am."* (John 14:1-4). To dwell in the house of the Lord forever.

CHAPTER 5. HOMECOMING SONG. PSALM 84

"How lovely is your dwelling place, O Lord Almighty! My soul yearns, even faints for the courts of the Lord; my heart and flesh cry out for the living God. Even the sparrow has found a home, and the swallow a nest for herself, where she may have her young – a place near your altar, O Lord God Almighty, my King and my God. Blessed are those who dwell in your house; they are ever praising you." (Psalm 84:1-4)

In our previous song we finished by reflecting on the fact that the Good Shepherd leads us to the place of an eternal home. Psalm 84 is a beautiful poem filled with the love and blessings of God towards his people. It is exemplified by the description of the dwelling place of the Lord and the invitation He gives to those who put their trust in Him. It is a place where the presence of God is and the place where his people from all walks of life will feel at home. Home is where the heart is. It's a place of belonging. A place of acceptance.

My place of belonging at one time was Glasgow; it was where my family home was. There was a time when I left Glasgow for three months working overseas and I missed my home, family and town so much. I would often sing: 'I belong to Glasgow, dear old Glasgow town. Well, what's the matter with Glasgow? For its goin' 'roon and 'roon. I'm only a common old working chap as anyone here can see. But when I get a couple of drinks on a Saturday, Glasgow belongs to me.'

We all want a place where we belong. A place of acceptance, of well-being and love. Home is more than a geographical place although that can be important. Home is where the heart is. My home for the last 21 years has been the Isle of Skye, it's a place where my wife and children live, it's a place where I am accepted in the community and it's a place where God has called me to be a minister of His Word. I am at home here because my heart is here! Psalm 84 is a prayer of longing for the house of the Lord. It is a place on Mount Zion in Jerusalem where the pilgrims would go up to the house of God singing songs of ascents, Psalms 120 to 134 during the gathering of the people for the festivals such as Passover and Pentecost.

It was a place where the exiled people would long to be and weep over as in Psalm 137, *"By the rivers of Babylon we sat and wept when we remembered Zion... Sing us one of the songs of Zion! How can we sing the songs of the Lord while in a foreign land?"* The people of Israel wanted to be home, their heart was not in Babylon, their worship centre was in another land. They did not belong in Babylon they belonged in Israel, Immanuel's land. They longed to be at the dwelling place of the Lord. *"My soul faints, for the courts of the Lord; my heart and flesh cry out for the living God. Even the sparrow has found a home, and the swallow a nest for herself."* (Psalm 84:2). This is an incredible verse when you think about it. God has a place near his altar even for the most insignificant thing! On a visit to Jerusalem, I went to the Western Wall and saw the incredible walls of the temple built with massive building blocks hewn out of rock, as I looked up at this vast structure my eyes were drawn to the little sparrows flying around and they were nesting in the crevices of these huge walls.

Jesus said that we were more valuable than sparrows, even the very hairs of our head are numbered, that is how much he loves us! Blessed are those who dwell in your house; they are ever praising you. We are blessed when we make our home, dwelling place in the residence of King Jesus. For the awesome revelation is; that He has come to make his home in our temporary dwelling. As Eugene Peterson wrote in his bible translation, the message, in John's Gospel chapter 1:14, 'The Word became flesh and blood, and moved into our neighbourhood.' or as the NIV puts it, *"The Word became flesh and made his dwelling among us."*

The dwelling of God is no longer confined to the temple in Jerusalem, it is extended into the human heart, into this flesh and blood. The Apostle Paul says that our body is the temple of the Holy Spirit. We are living stones and we can worship the Lord even in a foreign land. *"Better is one day in your courts than a thousand elsewhere; I would rather be a doorkeeper in the house of my God than dwell in the tents of the wicked."* (Psalm 84:10). We can still worship in a physical building with the people of God like the people of Israel whose great desire was to be in the presence of the Lord, and it is crucial for us to meet together in a building set apart for God as well as under the stars which is God's great outdoor cathedral. The amazing thing is that we are all individual houses of God and we are all door keepers to our hearts. God will never force himself in, he wants to be invited in to reside with us. The risen and ascended Jesus says, *"Here I am! I stand at the door and knock. If anyone hears my voice and opens the door, I will come in and eat with him, and he with me."* (Revelation 3:20). We are invited to a great homecoming. We are invited to journey home, and 'set our hearts on pilgrimage' back to our first love Jesus.

Jesus tells a story of a young man who was desperate to get away from home. He wanted to live life his way. He wanted away from his family and loving father to explore a world which seemed to offer him so much, if he had the money to fill his physical and material desires. The father in the story gives his share of the inheritance to this young son, who asked for it. The father shows so much love to his wayward son, gives him the share of his estate and lets him go! The son journeys to a distant land and spends his money in wild and riotous living. His money runs out, and his so-called new friends run out on him too! There is a famine within the land in which he lives, he is broke, no resources, no one to help him. He hires himself out to a pig farmer to feed pigs...for a young Jewish man that is the ultimate humiliation to feed (unclean animals) according to Jewish law. He has nothing to eat, his life is empty. His life has become like a pig sty, a mess and he is sinking! It is in the mud and mire of swine manure that he comes to his senses and remembers the love and generosity of his father. He sets out with a humbled heart, repents (about turn) on a journey that would lead him home. You see, home is where the heart is! Home is a place of welcome, acceptance and love. He knows the father's love but he does not realize how great that love is as he thinks he will become a servant rather than becoming a son!

"How great is the love the Father has lavished upon us that we should be called the children of God and that is what we are." (1 John 3:1)

What a homecoming! While he was still a long way off his father saw him and was filled with compassion for him; he ran to his son, threw his arms around him and kissed him.

This reminds me of a time I was working in Israel over the summer and I went to Tel Aviv airport to meet Helen who was coming to visit for two weeks. While I was waiting at the arrivals lounge my attention was drawn to this little Jewish boy who was quite excited that his dad was coming home. He kept saying 'Abba! Abba!' Which means 'dad' in Hebrew. I noticed that he started to get really excited and was jumping up and down as the arrivals door opened and he saw his dad. His dad saw him and started to run towards his son and the son came towards him. The father lifted him up and hugged him. All I could hear from the little boy was: 'Abba! Abba!' For me this was a picture of the Father's love as we see in the account of the lost son. He welcomes home the wayward son and embraces him with His love.

The Father's love knows no bounds, he lifts the lost son and reinstates him as a son, not a slave. He lifts him from the depths of despair to the place of deliverance. He does not impose on him the status of slave but rather the honour of being a son. *"My son,' the father said, 'you are always with me, and everything I have is yours. But we had to celebrate and be glad, because this brother of yours was dead and is alive again; he was lost and is found.'"* (Luke 15:31-32)

What a homecoming, a new set of clothes, a feast, a celebration, a wonderful welcome home! There is a homecoming song that is sung in heaven when a lost person comes home in repentance through faith in Jesus Christ. *"There is rejoicing in heaven over one sinner who repents than over ninety nine righteous persons who do not need to repent."* (Luke 15:7)

You unravel me with a melody, you surround me with a song

Of deliverance from my enemies, till all my fears are gone

From my mother's womb you have chosen me, Love has called my name.

I've been born again into a family, your blood flows through my veins.

I'm no longer a slave to fear, I am a child of God. (Bethel music 2014)

Welcome home! Welcome! Come on in and close the door. You've been gone so long. Welcome to your home once more!

CHAPTER 6. BATTLE SONG. PSALM 118

"Give thanks to the Lord, for he is good; his love endures forever."   (Psalm 118:1)

When armies go to war they usually have a battle song or battle cry. My first battle cry living in Glasgow whenever we faced opposition whether it was a fight or a football match was: 'Get in tae them!' Sadly, we will all have had to face a battle at one time or another. A battle over health, finance, faith, relationships, employment or unemployment. Many people have had to suffer two world wars and various battles and social unrest and the ongoing fight against Covid 19 in many countries to this day.

As Christians we are in a spiritual battle against the devil who is the enemy of Christ Jesus and these battles can manifest themselves in the physical as we may get opposition from people because of the faith we profess in Jesus Christ. Look at Ephesians 6.

I would like to take you to a battle that happened over 2,000 years ago and it came against God's people, the Israelites and their King Jehoshaphat, who were surrounded by enemies on every side!

A vast army of opposing forces came against Jehoshaphat; *"Alarmed, Jehoshaphat resolved to enquire of the Lord, and he proclaimed a fast for all Judah. The people of Judah came together to seek help from the Lord; indeed they came from every town in Judah to seek him."* (2 Chronicles 20:1-4). In other words King Jehoshaphat proclaimed a national time of prayer and fasting.

Eighty one years ago, the Dunkirk evacuation in World War II - also known as the Miracle of Dunkirk - was completed, saving over 300,000 troops. The initial operation, codenamed Operation Dynamo, was set in motion, but officials estimated that only a small number of the stranded troops - around 30,000 - would be able to be rescued. Ahead of the unfolding operation, King George VI called the people of Great Britain to a National Day of Prayer, on Sunday 26th May 1940. News coverage of the National Day of Prayer stated: 'It is well for us to show the world that we still believe in divine guidance [and] in the laws of Christianity; may we find inspiration and faith from this solemn day.' That very day, the evacuation began. Hundreds of boats set out across the English Channel in a rescue attempt, vulnerable to attack - but unseasonal storms meant Nazi air force were grounded and unable to fly. Additionally, Hitler had ordered his ground forces to halt, and they didn't move for three days. This combination of events meant that the evacuations were able to take place largely uninterrupted for three days, leading to over 338,000 men being rescued - ten times the expected number. The British Prime Minister, Winston Churchill called it a 'miracle of deliverance.'

King Jehoshaphat had come to the end of his tether when he said: *"O God, we have no power to face this vast army that is attacking us. We do not know what to do, but our eyes are upon you."* (2 Chronicles 20:12). He took the focus off himself and put his focus on God. Good leaders hide from the limelight and project the One who brings light!

God replies to his servant king through a prophetic word given by Jahaziel: *"Listen, King Jehoshaphat and all who live in Judah and Jerusalem! This is what the Lord says to you: 'Do not be afraid or discouraged because of this vast army. For the battle is not yours, but God's... You will not have to fight this battle. Take up your positions; stand firm and see the deliverance the Lord will give you... Have faith in the Lord your God and you will be upheld.'"* (2Chronicles 20:15-22)

Jehoshaphat appointed men to sing to the Lord and to praise him for the splendour of his holiness as they went out at the head of the army, saying: 'Give thanks to the Lord, for his love endures forever.'

There was no cry of 'Get in tae them!' They did not charge with guns and bullets or spears and swords. Their battle cry was a song of thanksgiving to the Lord and recognizing His great enduring love! This was their battle song that led them to a great victory over all their enemies. They did not have to lift a sword, spear any weapon to defeat the enemy, as they moved out they witnessed that the enemy had been defeated.

There is power in praise to demolish the enemy's strongholds. *"For though we live in this world, we do not wage war as the world does. The weapons we fight with are not the weapons of the world. On the contrary, they have divine power to demolish strongholds."* (2 Corinthians 10:3-4)

A great victory was achieved that day when a king humbled himself and gave the glory to the King of Heaven and went into the fight with a battle song that gave glory to the One and only who is full of grace and truth! The valley of fear became the Valley of Praise (Berakah) as the people rejoiced and praised the Lord, for He is good and His love endures forever. They returned to Jerusalem with great joy and thanksgiving with the sound of the harps, lutes and trumpets. *"And the kingdom of Jehoshaphat was at peace, for his God had given him rest on every side."* (2 Chronicles 20:30)

Psalm 118 is a battle song that gives thanks to the Lord for He is good and His love endures forever, woven through the song are these words from the first verse to the last verse and in between you read of the battle that the psalmist faced. He was in anguish...surrounded by enemies... pushed back and about to fall. But the Lord helped me. The Lord is my strength and my song; he has become my salvation.

This song is also prophetic as it looked to a time when the coming Messiah Jesus would be rejected by some but embraced by others. He is our salvation, He is our song of deliverance, He is our conquering king overcoming death and the work of the devil. His kingdom is unshakable because it is an eternal kingdom that can impact the lives of people who believe in Jesus the Messiah but there are some who reject this living stone. *"The stone the builders rejected has become the capstone; the Lord has done this and it is marvellous in our eyes. This is the day that the Lord has made; let us rejoice and be glad in it."* (v 22-24)

Our nation lives in uncertain times, the very fabric of our nation is crumbling under the pressure of many enemies to the gospel of Jesus Christ. Our moral standards and our Judaic/Christian heritage and values are under attack. Sadly, we are living in a nation where many have turned their back on the church and we can understand why because we have become judgmental towards the so called sinners in our society often condemning them and their lifestyle without showing any grace, love, hope and forgiveness. There has also been a rise in militant secularists groups who oppose the gospel and the preaching of the gospel in our towns, villages and cities.

It is time for the believers in Jesus to raise the battle cry! To praise, pray and proclaim the good news to our nation again.

Our battle song is a new song of grace and mercy to the broken, bruised, rejected, beaten and our enemies in our communities. It is a song that the enemy cannot triumph over. It is a song that is different from the world's songs and the armies of this world. It's a song of thanksgiving and love. It has the power to demolish strongholds over lives.

Give thanks to the Lord our God and king, his love endures forever.

For He is good He is above all things, His love endures forever.

Sing praise! Sing praise!

From the rising to the setting sun, His love endures forever.

And by the grace of God we will carry on. His love endures forever!

With a mighty hand and an outstretched arm, His love endures forever.

For the life that has been re-born, His love endures forever!

(Forever, song by Chris Tomlin)

Give thanks to the Lord, for He is good, his love endures forever!

Raise the banner of Jesus high. He is the hope of our nation! He has won the victory over death, demonic and oppressive forces of evil. In an act of love. Love breaks the back of sin! Love conquers all. Love is the greatest thing! Love is personified in Jesus! His love endures forever! That is our battle song! The new song that can give you victory over sin, evil, wickedness and death! His love is eternal because it endures forever!

CHAPTER 7. BIRTHDAY
SONG. PSALM 139

Everybody has a day they were taken from their mother's womb to be born into this world. Usually we all celebrate that day once a year by being sung to with the words: 'Happy birthday to you...' with your name in the third verse of the song. Our birthday is usually a celebration to give thanks for our coming into the world. The Bible shares a lot about 'birth' and 'birthdays.' One of the incredible songs in scripture was written by King David, Psalm 139 where he describes the miracle of our conception and birth.

"For you created my inmost being; you knit me together in my mother's womb. I praise you because I am fearfully and wonderfully made; your works are wonderful, I know that full well. My frame was not hidden from you when I was made in the secret place." (v13-15)

Before ultrasound scans God revealed to David the incredible miracle of life that is created, woven together in the secret place. You are not a mistake, you were created and formed by God. *"Woven together in the depths of the earth, your eyes saw my unformed body. All the days ordained for me were written in your book before one of them came to be."* (v15-16). Life begins even before the womb in the depths of the earth, we are created from dust as our first parents Adam and Eve (Genesis 2:7, Ephesians 1:4) but through procreation God created our inmost being and knit us together in our mother's womb. We are fearfully and wonderfully made!

The word of God also reveals to us that although God has created us in His image, there is another birth which takes place in a believer's life. It is called 'new birth' 'born again' or 'born from above.' Jesus in John's gospel chapter three that great chapter in which is found: *"For God so loved the world that he gave his one and only son that whosoever believes in him should not perish but have eternal life."* (v16). This is said after Jesus had challenged a very religious man, Israel's teacher, Nicodemus on what it meant to be a follower of God. Jesus declared, *"I tell you the truth, no-one can see the kingdom of God unless he is born-again."* (v3). Nicodemus does not understand Jesus, he replies 'How can a man be born when he is old?... Surely he cannot enter his mother's womb a second time to be born?' Jesus answered, 'I tell you the truth no one can enter the kingdom of God unless he is born of water and the Spirit.'

There must be a 'wind of change' in your heart and mind, revelation of God's word and Spirit, dying to self and being born again through faith in the work of Jesus Christ on the cross to save you from your sin, and belief in the resurrection of Christ from the dead and His ascension into heaven. He has sent the Holy Spirit who comes and brings life in all its fullness. Through His word and Spirit in Jesus Christ we are made new! New creations, where the old has gone and the new has come. This is the experience that Peter had when he wrote and sang this powerful birthday song.

"Praise be to the God and Father of our Lord Jesus Christ! In his great mercy he has given us new birth into a living hope through the resurrection of Jesus Christ from the dead, and into an inheritance that can never perish, spoil or fade - kept in heaven for you, who through faith are shielded by God's power until the coming of salvation that is ready to be revealed in the last time." (1Peter 1:3-5)

This birthday song is one of thanksgiving, hope, faith and the assurance of a heavenly gift that we are to inherit. An inheritance that can never perish, spoil or fade. Jesus said something about storing up for yourself treasures in heaven. *"Do not store up for yourselves treasures on earth, where moth and rust destroy, and where thieves break in and steal. But store up for yourselves treasures in heaven, where moth and rust do not break in steal. For where your treasure is, there your heart will be also."* (Matthew 5:19-21)

Before we sing a new song or for that matter a new birthday song we need to ask: 'What does it mean to be born again?' Billy Graham writes in his book, How to be Born Again: 'Born again is not a remodeling job, performed somehow by us on ourselves. Today we hear a lot about

recycling, reconstruction, and reshaping. We renovate houses and add on more rooms. We tear down old buildings and build new ones in our cities, calling it urban renewal. Millions and millions of pounds are spent every year on health spas, beauty salons, and exotic cosmetics - all by people hoping to reshape their faces or renew their bodies.

In like manner, people frantically pursue all sorts of promised cures for the renewal of their inner lives. Some people hunt for renewal at the psychiatrist's office. Others search for spiritual renewal in exotic oriental religions or processes of inward meditation. Still others seek for inner peace and renewal in drugs or alcohol. Whatever the path however, they eventually come to a dead end. Why? Simply because people cannot renew themselves. God created us. Only God can recreate us! Only God can give us the new birth we so desperately want and need.'

New birth in Christ offers us more than we can imagine. Eternal riches, spiritual and physical renewal, a new heart and a new way of thinking. It is a transformation of body, mind and spirit.

I believe that the central theme of the universe is the purpose and destiny of every individual. Every person is important in God's eyes. The greatest news in the universe is that we can be born again! Because God gave his son Jesus as an act of love to pay the price for all our sin and wrongdoing, He died on the cruel cross of Calvary our sin put Him on that cross, but it was not the end, He defeated sin, death and the grave and rose victoriously on the third day! If you confess with your mouth that Jesus is Lord and believe in your heart that God raised him from the dead, you will be saved. New creations! Born from above! Born again!

Today I found myself after searching all these years, and

GARY WILSON

the man that I saw he wasn't at all who I thought he'd be

I was lost when you found me here, I was broken beyond repair, then you came along and you sang your song over me.

It feels like I'm born again, it feels like I'm living, for the very first time. (Third day: Born again 2008)

CHAPTER 8. HAPPY SONG. PSALM 100

Someone said; 'The pursuit of happiness is the great obsession of humanity.' If you look up happiness quotes on Google you are overwhelmed with pages and pages of sayings.

Charlotte Bronte writes: 'There is no happiness like that of being loved by your fellow creatures, and feeling that your presence is an addition to their comfort.'

Aristotle defined happiness: 'Happiness is the meaning and purpose of life, the whole aim and end of human existence.'

But do these quotes reflect the biblical idea of the word happy? The first time one finds happy in the Bible, it was about family... a mother naming a child after the happiness she felt when he was born. We find this in Genesis 30:12-13; *"Then Leah said, 'How happy I am! The women will call me happy.' So she named him Asher."* So the Hebrew word for happy is 'asher' it can also mean blessed although there is another Hebrew word for blessed 'barak.'

Psalm 112:1-2 *"Praise the Lord. Blessed/happy (asher) is the man who fears the Lord, who finds great delight in his commands."*

Psalm 1:1-2 *"Happy (asher)/blessed is the man who does not walk in the counsel of the wicked or stand in the way of sinners or sit in the seat of mockers. But his delight is in the law of the Lord, and on his law he meditates day and night."*

Many of the psalms are joyful, exuberant worship and praise songs to Almighty God, as they come out of our relationship with God. Psalm 150 starts by using the word: 'Hallelujah!' Which is a Hebrew word meaning; 'Praise the Lord.' This song is almost a command for 'everything that has breath to praise the Lord.'

Why? For His acts of power. For His surpassing greatness!

How? With musical instruments, dancing and singing!

He is the Almighty God. Look at his acts of creation. Look at the power by which He raised Christ Jesus from the dead. Experience the saving touch of Jesus and the flames of power through the Holy Spirit that revives and renews our life and our walk with God. We have something to be happy about.

As Tim Hughes wrote:

Greatest day in history, death defeated you have rescued me, sing it out Jesus is alive.

The empty cross the empty grave, life eternal you have won the day, sing it out Jesus is alive, he is alive!

Oh, happy day, you washed my sin away, I will never be the same, forever I am changed!

"Shout for joy to the Lord, all the earth. Worship the Lord

with gladness; come before him with joyful songs. Know that the Lord is God. It is he who made us, and we are his; we are his people, the sheep of his pasture." (Psalm 100:1-2)

I find it very strange that in some church denominations their service can be very dull and sombre. I remember leading worship one morning in a church and we were singing; 'O Happy day when Jesus washed my sins away! And live rejoicing every day, Hallelujah! Happy Day!' As I looked at the congregation they did not look very happy singing that song, in fact I probably did not look too happy myself. I felt the Spirit prompting me to stop and reflect on the words we were singing and how we were singing them. I was challenged to reflect from my face and heart a bit of joy instead of it being like a funeral dirge. We decided to sing the song again and what a difference the second time around. We were thinking about what we were singing and giving thanks to God and the joy of the Lord shone from our faces!

The word 'happy' in the New Testament is closely related with the word 'blessed' which is a Greek word 'Makarios,' which can mean both words. Jesus taught in the beatitudes that people who were; poor in spirit, mourning, meek, merciful, seeking after righteousness, pure in heart, peacemakers, persecuted would be 'blessed,' 'happy'. This is not walking around all day with a big cheesy grin and inside you are falling apart. This kind of happiness is deep, it helps us in our struggles and times of adversity, it gives us strength, the joy of the Lord is our strength. It is having peace and contentment in all situations, whether well fed or hungry, whether living in plenty or in want. I can do everything through him who gives me strength. (Philippians 4:13)

The psalmist continues: *"Enter his gates with thanksgiving and his courts with praise; give thanks to him and praise his name. For the Lord is good and his love endures forever; his faithfulness continues through all generations."*

Real excitement in our worship and praise to God. We can do it in our quiet places, out in the fields, mountains, gardens, gatherings of people and everywhere there is breath, Praise the Lord!

The joy of the Lord is our strength. Joy in the most difficult in the challenging situations we may face. Know that He is greater and that He is good and His love endures forever. Our problems will not endure forever they come for a time, only one thing endures forever and that is God's love towards you!

Our relationship with God is what brings us deep lasting happiness as well as our healthy relationships with others. Ultimate happiness has a connection to relationship and family and that is the joy of knowing that when we are in pursuit of God we find real happiness because He also is in pursuit of us. Remember the words of Jesus to a religious hypocrite: *"I tell you that in the same way there will be more rejoicing in heaven over one sinner who repents than other ninety-nine righteous persons who do not need to repent."* (Luke 15:7)

Our Abba/Father is happy when a person is 'born again' into His family and we know that deep inner joy that comes from heaven impacting our lives through the power of the Holy Spirit in Jesus name!

When I stand in that place, free at last, meeting face to face.

I am yours, Jesus, you are mine, endless joy, perfect peace.

Earthly pain finally will cease, celebrate, Jesus is alive, He's alive.

Oh, happy day, happy day, you washed my sins away, Oh happy day, happy day, I'll never be the same, forever I am changed.

(Tim Hughes)

CHAPTER 9. FAITH SONG. PSALM 127

"Unless the Lord builds the house, its builders labour in vain. Unless the Lord watches over the city, the watchmen stand guard in vain."   (Psalm 127:1-2)

These songs are taken from a section of the psalms that are called: 'Songs of Ascents' from Psalm 120 to Psalm 134. They were sung by the pilgrims as they ascended up to the Temple in Jerusalem, which is built on a mountain called Zion, to worship God. Its themes are timeless; it reminded the pilgrims on their way to Jerusalem that all of life's securities and blessings are gifts from God rather than their own achievements. In other words, no amount of human sacrifice or toil can accomplish much unless God's blessing is upon His people. 'Unless the Lord builds the house, the builders labour in vain.'

A few months ago, I was watching a demolition team come in and knock down old housing flats in Portree. These guys demolished in a few days what it took engineers and builders years to construct. This song is reminding us that it is futile to build anything in this life if it is not given over to God. The things that humanity builds do not last forever. We can construct great structures, we can build amazing houses, we can build our lives on wealth and material pleasures but they do not last forever. Look at the grandeur of the Roman Empire if you can see it, where is it now? The power and advancement of the British Empire, where has it gone? The psalmist is reminding the people what happened to them when they took God out of their everyday life! Catastrophe! Destruction and demolition of society.

God has called his people to be builders but to look at His plans for society. The welfare of society is benefitted when it is built upon a solid foundation of God and the obedience to His Word.

Jesus tells the story of two house builders in Matthew 7:24-27 who both had the same materials and same skills but one chose the right location, and the other chose the wrong one. One was foolish as he tried to do it the easy way by constructing his house on the sand. Yes it was close to the beach. Yes it had great views and would be a number one contender for Airbnb customers but it was greatly flawed. The foundation was dodgy and when a storm hit, the structure crumbled and crashed to the ground and was taken away by the raging sea in a moment! On the other hand, the wise man in the story built his house on the rock and when the storm hit the structure, it stood firm because it was built on a good and solid foundation. Jesus told this story in relation to challenging people as to what they are building their lives upon. We are all building our lives on something; however is it something that lasts forever or for a short time?

What are you building your life upon? Your status? Your success? Your wealth? Your homes, cars, jobs?

Jesus taught another parable about a man who tore

down his barns to build bigger ones to store all his riches for a rainy day. He thought I will take life easy, eat, drink and be merry. *"But God said to him, 'You fool! This very night your life will be demanded from you. Then who will get what you have prepared for yourself?' This is how it will be with anyone who stores up things for himself but is not rich towards God."* (Luke 12:13-21)

The author of Psalm 127 was King Solomon and he knew to his cost the folly of building vast empires, having so much wealth and material pleasures, he had everything that a person would desire, everything he set his eyes upon was his but he writes: *" I undertook great projects: I built houses for myself and planted vineyards. I made gardens and parks and planted all kinds of fruit trees in them. I made reservoirs to water groves of flourishing trees. I bought male and female slaves and had other slaves who were born in my house. I also owned more herds and flocks than anyone in Jerusalem before me. I amassed silver and gold for myself, and the treasures of the kings and provinces. I acquired men and women singers, and a harem as well - the delights of the heart of man. I became greater by far than anyone in Jerusalem before me. In all this my wisdom stayed with me.*

I denied myself nothing my eyes desired; I refused my heart no pleasure. My heart took delight in all my work, and this was the reward of all my labour. Yet when I surveyed all that my hands had done and what I toiled to achieve, everything was meaningless, a chasing after the wind; nothing was gained under the sun." (Ecclesiastes 2:4-11)

Whenever we take God out of the equation, everything is meaningless a chasing after the wind. You see our life is not about how much money we have or the letters we have after our name. It's not about how we look or what clothes we wear, styles and fashion. It's not about where we live or what we do. It's about 'whose' we are? Who is on the throne of our heart?

It's not wrong to have great projects, or build houses and have amazing recreational time. It's about who we put first in our lives.

Jesus said to a people who were seeking after meaning and purpose in life, a people who were worried about many things: *"Therefore I tell you, do not worry about your life, what you will eat or drink; or about your body, what you will wear. Is not life more important than food, and the body more important than clothes? Look at the birds of the air; they do not sow or reap or store away in barns, and yet your heavenly Father feeds them. Are you not much more valuable than they?...Seek first the kingdom of God and his righteousness and all of these things will be given to you as well."* (Matthew 6:25-34)

Unless the Lord is involved in our daily lives, in our home, work, family life, community projects and ministries then we labour in vain. However, if we build our life on the Lord Jesus Christ, His Word, His Way, His Worship, we are building on a good and solid foundation for as you do so you will find the 'Heavenly builder' is constructing something of His kingdom within you that will have an impact on everything we do. It will bring hope to the hopeless, light to the darkness, love to the unloved, wholeness to the brokenness, and peace to the troubled heart.

As the Rend collective song proclaims:

Build your kingdom here, let the darkness fear.

Show your mighty hand, heal our streets and land.

Set your church on fire, bring this nation back.

Change the atmosphere, build your kingdom here, we pray!

Therefore everyone who hears these words of mine and puts them into practice is like a wise man who built his house on the rock. This is our faith song, a song that puts God first in all that we do and say. A song that believes that when we do so, we will see the kingdom of God at work bringing about his love and presence, into the lives of others in the advancement of the kingdom in our homes, communities and nation!

CHAPTER 10. MOUNTAIN SONG. PSALM 121

"I lift up my eyes to the hills, where does my help come from? My help comes from the Lord the Maker of heaven and earth."   (Psalm 121:1-2)

I have lived on the beautiful Isle of Skye for the past 21 years. I am truly blessed to live in such a stunning landscape. At the heart of Skye lies the dominant feature of the majestic mountain peaks of the Black Cuillin. In fact at Sligachan hotel there is a viewfinder naming all the mountain peaks you can see by looking up to the hills. Also written on it in Gaelic are the words from Psalm 121. I lift up my eyes to the hills. It is an incredible spot to see these powerful mountains, they are some of the most dangerous peaks in the British Isles. I can picture the psalmist looking up to the hills surrounding Jerusalem and being overwhelmed by their stature and height and thinking and singing: I lift up my eyes to the hills, where does my help come from?

For many ancient people the high places were the places where God was to be found. You can read many accounts in the Bible of God meeting with Moses on Mount Sinai, Elijah on Mount Carmel, Jesus on the Mount of Transfiguration, psalmist meditating on Mount Hermon (Psalm 133). The psalmist reminds himself and all the pilgrims who would ascend up to Jerusalem to celebrate one of the Festivals of the Lord, that this song was not about finding your help from the mountains, rather finding your help in the One who created the mountains. The Lord the Maker of heaven and earth. God is bigger than the mountains. He is incomparable to any living creature or act of creation because He is the One who fashioned the moon and the stars and set them in place. What is man that you are mindful of him, the son of man that you care for him? (Psalm 8)

Those singing this worship song heading up the mountain are people whose hope and faith are in the Lord. This song is about a God who is not distant and living in the clouds, this God is near to us. Five times they sing about God 'watching over them.' He who watches over you will not slumber, He who watches over Israel will neither slumber nor sleep.

This is a beautiful picture of a loving parent watching over their child. I remember when our children were youngsters we would put them to bed and from time to time while they were asleep we would go into their room to check on them to make sure they were alright, in other words we watched over them while they were asleep. They had the assurance that mum and dad would be looking after them and keeping them safe during the watches of the night. The psalmist is saying even in the most unsusceptible times of life, when we are at our most vulnerable, the Lord watches over us. He guards us in our most unguarded time!

'The word 'watch' is from the Hebrew root word 'shamar' which means to watch or keep. It also means to guard, preserve, and keep safe. The word shamar has one more element to it that is often overlooked. The word shamar in extra-biblical literature is used for a diamond or something that is so precious, so glowing that you cannot take your eyes off of it. You see, when the psalmist is telling us that God shamars us, he is saying that He is doing more than just watching over us, He is admiring us as something so precious that He will guard it with His life.' (Chaim Bentorah, Biblical Hebrew Studies, by Chaim and Laura Oct 2013)

The Lord will keep you from all harm, He will watch over your life; the Lord will watch over your coming and going both now and for evermore.

On a visit to Israel I visited some Jewish friends and I noticed that on the posts/frame of their doors they had a beautiful ornament fixed to the door posts. I was intrigued as to what this was. They informed me that it was not an ornament, rather it was a 'mezuzah' which contained a portion of the scriptures, Hebrew Bible. These stunningly decorated mezuzah are attached to the doorposts as literally described in the book of Deuteronomy 6:4-9 which says: "*These commandments I give you today are to be upon your hearts... write them on the door frames of your houses and on your gates.*" When people leave their homes they touch the mezuzah and also when they come back home. It is not superstitious, it is thanking God and reminding them that the Lord watches over their comings and goings both now and forever more!

As the pilgrims looked up to the mountains and saw the strength and beauty of these peaks it made them look beyond to the One who is Creator and sustainer of all things. It also made them look at their own vulnerabilities and by faith in the Lord believed that the same God who created the universe is the same God who is called Immanuel, God with us. In all our comings and goings both now and forever more.

We can touch the word of God today by reading it and experiencing His presence with us through the Counsellor the Holy Spirit. We can know that God is with us because the Word became flesh and made His dwelling among us full of grace and truth. (John 1:14). This is the mountain song that we can sing! This is the song of assurance that God is for us and not against us.

Look beyond the mountain, the circumstances you face, the rejection you may feel, the emotional and physical pain you may be in, to the One who went through the valley of pain, rejection and hatred, who carried all the burdens and sin of the world with a cross on His back to a mountain called Calvary. He overcame all that the enemy could throw at him by rising beyond the mountain on the third day and bringing life beyond the grave. Jesus is the resurrection and the life! The hope of glory! The King of kings and the Lord of lords. This is our mountain song; 'Our Help comes from the Lord the Maker of heaven and earth... He will watch over your life; the Lord will watch over your coming and going both now and for evermore.'

CHAPTER 11. SOUL SONG. PSALM 103

"Praise the Lord O my soul; all my inmost being, praise his Holy name. Praise the Lord O my soul, and forget not all his benefits - who forgives all your sins and heals all your diseases, who redeems your life from the pit and crowns you with love and compassion." (Psalm 103:1-4)

'Soul music is a combination of R&B (Rhythm and Blues) and gospel music and began in the late 1950s in the United States. While soul has a lot in common with R&B, its differences include the use of gospel music, its greater emphasis on vocalists, and merging of religious and secular themes.' (Mark Edward Nero 2018)

Soul music, soul songs had its origins way before the 1950s to more than 2000 years ago, found in the book of Psalms the song of David number 103 is the very essence of soul and a man giving his all, pouring out his passion and singing with all his heart, mind and soul. This soul song is about his relationship with God and God's relationship with David. Before we look at this song we should ask the question: What is the meaning of soul?

The Hebrew word for 'soul' is 'nephesh' which occurs over 700 times in the Old Testament and its meaning is the whole person, living, breathing, physical being. When David sings 'Praise the Lord, O my soul;' he is using the word nephesh which means my whole being, body, mind and spirit! With everything, my flesh, my intellect, my inner spirit, my heart, my all, Praise the Lord!

This deep soulful song is a cry from the heart but also a declaration of faith in his God who has done great things in his life.

He forgives all your sins... He heals all your diseases... He redeems your life from the pit... He crowns you with love and compassion... He satisfies your desires with good things... He is compassionate and gracious... His love is everlasting... He is the king over all.

This is a soul song that comes from the whole being which has been moved and touched by the compassion and unfailing love of God. Modern day soul songs are more a search for meaning and purpose to life whereas this Song of David has been written and expressed in words that have found their ultimate goal, purpose and existence in this life which is having a relationship with the loving Creator of his soul.

This soul song is a new song that comes from the very recesses of your being. It's a new song that develops through life's trials and tribulations, joys and victories. The new song is an anthem of our soul that is connected to the Lord of hosts who has stepped down from the heavenly realms to put on our flesh and blood in the form of the Messiah Jesus! It is through his sacrifice and victory song from the cross; 'It is finished!' (complete, whole, wellbeing) that we have a new song to sing and hymn of praise to our God. For he has lifted us up from the mud and mire of this life and has set our feet upon a rock and gave me a firm place to stand. He put a new song in my mouth, a hymn of praise to our God. Many will see and fear and put their trust in the Lord.

This new song is more than a verbal outpouring of praise and thanksgiving to God. It is a song that has a transforming change to our whole being as many will not just hear it but will see the outworking of it in a radically changed life, where the old has gone and the new creation is formed. Many will see and fear and put their trust in the Lord.

This new song has its beginnings with Almighty God, our loving heavenly Father who imparts a love song over his children. He is the very source of the new song that we sing. The prophet Zephaniah writes:

"The Lord your God is with you, he is mighty to save. He will take great delight in you, he will quiet you with his love, he will rejoice over you with singing."

Rejoice! Rejoice! Christ is in you, the hope of glory in our hearts. He lives, He lives, His breath is in you arise a mighty army we arise!

Arise O people of God and sing a new song of love and salvation, sing it over your children, over your community, over your family and over your nation that many will see and fear and put their trust in the Lord.

CHAPTER 12. HALLELUJAH
SONG. PSALM 150

The last five songs in the book of Psalms are called the Hallelujah songs! The opening verse and closing verse of each psalm have the Hebrew word; 'Hallelujah' which in English is the phrase 'Praise the Lord'.

I often hear this word Hallelujah being branded around in all sorts of situations and among all sorts of people. One day when I was taking an assembly in my local primary school I asked the children if they had heard or even said the word 'Hallelujah,' the majority of them had. When I asked if they knew what it meant the answers were very different as to the meaning! Some did not know! Some thought it was something you say if you get good news or are happy! Some have heard it in the media when people win something or if you have passed your exams, got a new job or have escaped a near miss, or your team has not lost.

Many can use words without knowing what they really mean. When I explained to the children that the verse means 'Praise the Lord' some were shocked! 'Hallel' means Praise and 'Jah' means God or the Lord!

There are a lot of people saying Hallelujah, praising God without realizing what they are saying. The psalmist, songwriter, knew what he was singing, he had a new song in his mouth it was a Hallelujah song, a praise the

Lord song to the King of kings and the Lord of lords! This God is to be glorified, magnified and praised for who He is and not just with the singing voice but also with musical instruments. The whole of creation is to raise a Hallelujah to the Creator, Saviour of the universe. The angels, heavenly hosts, sun, moon, shining stars, skies, sea creatures, lightning, hail, snow, clouds, winds, mountains, trees, birds, creatures, kings, rulers, men and women, children. (Psalm 148). Everything that has breath praise the Lord. (Psalm 150)

We are to praise His name with dancing, with the tambourine and harp, strings and flute, cymbals and lyre. (Psalm 149-150)

Why are we called to praise the Lord? For His acts of power and for His surpassing greatness, for He is our king! *"He has revealed his word to Jacob, his laws and decrees to Israel."* (Psalm 147:19)

He upholds the cause of the oppressed and gives food to the hungry, He sets prisoners free, gives sight to the blind, lifts up the humble, sustains the fatherless and the widow... The Lord reigns forever... Hallelujah! (Psalm 146:7-10)

When you are filled with the Holy Spirit and transformed by the love of Jesus and stand in awe before the Heavenly Father then you are the singer of a new song, a Hallelujah song!

We join in with the angels in heaven. And they sang a new song:

"'You are worthy to take the scroll and to open its seals, because you were slain, and with your blood you purchased men for God persons from every tribe and language and people and nation. You have made them to be a kingdom and priests to serve our God, and they will reign on the earth.' Then I looked and heard the voice of many angels, numbering thousands upon thousands, and ten thousand times ten thousand... In a loud voice they sang: 'Worthy is the Lamb, who was slain, to receive power, wealth and wisdom and strength and honour and glory and praise!'" (Revelation 5:9-12)

In one of the most challenging and uncertain moments of Joel and Janie Taylor's life a song was born in the midst of a family crisis. It was a Hallelujah song. The Taylor's two year old son, Jaxon had taken ill, his kidneys were closing down due to an E-coli virus attacking his organs, whilst suffering from seizures and respiratory issues things were looking very bleak. Soon after, their four year old daughter Addie was diagnosed with the same infection. Faced with the possible loss of their son and daughter, the couple cried out to their community for prayer and support.

Their story was shared on Instagram, as Christians from all over the world joined in prayer and intercession for the Taylors. Worship leaders and friends Jonathan and Melissa Helser, were in constant contact with the Taylors and received news one night from the Taylors that they did not think Jaxon would make it through the night. 'As soon as I got that text, I felt like this giant of unbelief stood in front of me,' Jonathan Helser said. 'I thought Jaxon is going to die tonight, we're not going to see the miracle.'

As the Helsers started to pray for Jaxon, a new song came out. 'All of a sudden, out of my gut, this song came out in the face of the giant – I raise a hallelujah, in the presence of my enemies. I raise a hallelujah, louder than the unbelief.' This song became an anthem for the Taylors throughout the rest of the battle for Jaxon's life. Making worship their weapon, more friends from the community came to the hospital, numerous treatments and countless prayers, the Taylors were allowed to go home with two healthy children.

Joel Taylor recounts his experience, 'God's timing often doesn't make sense until you look back to see that mountains were climbed and canyons were crossed in no strength of your own. In the battle for Jaxon's life, the global church community rose up like a mighty army and joined us in prayer and worship all over the world. Our son was miraculously healed and today is perfectly healthy.'

I raise a hallelujah, in the presence of my enemies

I raise a hallelujah, louder than the unbelief

I raise a hallelujah, my weapon is a melody

I raise a hallelujah, heaven comes to fight for me.

I'm gonna sing, in the middle of the storm, louder and louder, you're gonna hear my praises roar. Up from the ashes hope will arise, death is defeated, the King is alive.

I raise a hallelujah, with everything inside of me

I raise a hallelujah, I will watch the darkness flee

I raise a hallelujah, in the middle of the mystery

I raise a hallelujah, fear you lost your hold on me.

(Jonathan and Melissa Helser. Bethel music)

In the middle of a storm a new song came out, a song that faces the giants of this world. It is a hallelujah song that praises the Lord in the middle of the conflict. It is a hallelujah song that is real, faithful and true. It is a hallelujah song that is full of love, thanksgiving and deliverance.

"Hallelujah, Praise the Lord, O my soul, I will praise the Lord all of my life; I will sing praise to my God as long as I live. Do not put your trust in princes, in mortal men, who cannot save... Blessed is he whose help is in the God of Jacob, whose help is in the Lord his God the Maker of heaven and earth. Hallelujah! Praise the Lord!" (Psalm 146)

Printed in Great Britain
by Amazon